BRITAIN IN OLD PHOTOGRAPHS

STRETFORD

CLIFF & SYLVIA HAYES

SUTTON PUBLISHING LIMITED

Sutton Publishing Limited
Phoenix Mill · Thrupp · Stroud
Gloucestershire · GL5 2BU

First published 1997

Title page photograph: the Old Cottages,
Mitford Street, Stretford.

British Library Cataloguing in Publication Data
A catalogue record for this book is available from the
British Library.

ISBN 0-7509-1690-7

Typeset in 10/12 Perpetua.
Typesetting and origination by
Sutton Publishing Limited.
Printed in Great Britain by
Ebenezer Baylis, Worcester.

Chester Road, Stretford, 1968. A few months later it was cleared away for road widening work to begin.
This photograph was taken from roughly where the bus shelter for Sale and Altrincham is today. None of
these shops survived and shopping in Stretford has changed for ever.

CONTENTS

ACKNOWLEDGEMENTS

Of all the many people who contributed to this book my biggest thanks must go to Bill Newton, the librarian and historian, who kindly allowed me to plunder his 'box of bits' – without his generosity many of these photographs would not be included here; he also supplied the photographs for the Postscript section. Thanks are also due to Stretford Local History Society, a very active and worthwhile body, for the loan of a number of postcards, and to the now defunct *Stretford and Urmston Journal* which donated their photographs to the Society; to Ted Grey for the horse-tram and tram photographs and information; to Gordon Coltas (Locofotos) for permission to reproduce his impressive steam train pictures; to everyone in the libraries, churches and streets of Stretford who answered my hundreds of questions; and lastly a very special thank you is due to my lovely wife Sylvia who typed and corrected the manuscript.

The Stretford Local History Society was born on 18 February 1982 when Mr W. Newton, the Senior Assistant Librarian for Trafford Library Services, chaired a meeting attended by eleven residents of Stretford and several representatives of the thriving Urmston Local History Society and Hulme History Society. Fifteen years later, it is now a part of Stretford life. It has put on exhibitions and produced magazines, and holds more than 2,500 slides and an even larger number of other illustrations depicting Stretford's past. The Society meets on the third Thursday of each month at 7.30 p.m. in Stretford Public Hall (side entrance), and anyone interested in the area's history is welcome to attend. More details are available from Stretford Public Library.

INTRODUCTION

In 1972 the Local Government Bill became law, forcing Stretford, Sale, Urmston, Altrincham, Hale, Bowdon and parts of Bucklow to join together as a single administrative unit, containing some 230,000 people and considerable variety, with money in the south and overcrowding in the north. No one area dominated and various combinations of the names of the areas, such as 'Alt-Urm-Stret', 'Stretflixham' and 'Altrinflix' were considered before it became obvious that a single new name was needed. Trafford was put forward and finally adopted. The Trafford family, who had once owned and ruled much of the area, took their name from the area at Trafford Bar; their name now lends itself to the whole of the MBC.

The name Stretford is derived from a very simple base. The Romans built a paved road, a *streta*, between Chester and Manchester. They were not keen on bridge-building, and when they came to a river they would cut back the banks, lower the river level and create a ford. Their crossing point was 'Crossford Bridge', a fascinating area even today. Stretford is the place where the *streta* fords the river. Later Saxon settlers did not alter the name. Stretford is not mentioned in the Domesday Book, but by the mid-fifteenth century there is a reference to a hamlet and an inn called the Bishop Blaize. Blaize was the patron saint of woolcombers, the derivation suggesting that there may have been sheep farms in the area.

Opinions differ concerning the name Trafford. It may come from the same source as Stretford. It could have started out as *Streta*-Ford and lost the initial 'S'. It may be derived from the Welsh word Trefan, meaning an abode, and hence Tref-ford, the abode by the ford. Some history books say Trafford is derived from Tri-ford, the three fords, but I think this is unlikely as it was hard work keeping a ford in good order. The river-bed at the crossing would need to be firmed and the banks repaired, and travellers would need assistance; it would be extra hard work with three fords.

The coming of the Bridgewater Canal was the next major upheaval in the Stretford area. The canal reached Taylor's Bridge, Stretford, around 1762, and it was the building of the canal at Throstle's Nest, now Trafford Bar, that forced the Trafford family out of Trafford Hall (around what is now the police headquarters in Boyer Street). The family moved into its country seat, Trafford Park, and rebuilt the manor/farm house called

Whittleswick Hall. The area they left behind became known as Old Trafford (Hall), and the name stuck as Old Trafford.

Because produce could get to Manchester faster on the new Bridgewater Canal, there was money to be made from this new venture and although the Duke made most of it, there was still some for the 'locals'. Farms grew up around Stretford, sending their produce into Manchester. The area was especially noted for its pig farms, pork and its by-products, and was nicknamed 'Porkhampton'. It was also noted for the production of rhubarb, nicknamed 'Stretford Beef', which thrived on pig manure.

The area known as Stretford in the early 1800s was merely a collection of farms above the River Mersey, around Chester Road, Chapel Lane and Higgin Lane (now Barton Road). It was never actually a quaint old-fashioned type of village. The few buildings – farmhouses, workers' cottages and the odd pub – were widely scattered. There is some evidence of a sort of 'village green' off Chester Road, near Edge Lane corner, but nothing very permanent.

The arrival of the Manchester, South Junction & Altrincham Railway in 1849, and the ever widening boundaries of Manchester, sparked off the second development of the Stretford area. Old Trafford was, and still is, a unique area, very different from old Stretford. Its tightly-packed streets and houses sprang up over a century ago, and all the road names have a connection with the de Trafford family. The area reaches almost to Brooks's Bar and Moss Side, granted by that family. The bordering Whalley Range and Brooks's Bar were both begun by Samuel Brooks with his plan for another 'Victoria Park' of villas in a select up-market development. To the east are Chorlton and Longford Park, a controversial area, at one time home of one of Stretford's benefactors, John Rylands. To the west is Urmston and, of course, the boundary included about half of Trafford Park.

Around 1750 Stretford was an area of fewer than 1,500 acres. The Vestry committee, with its Church connections, and Overseers and Guardians put in place by the (de) Trafford family ran the day-to-day life of the village. The Local Board took over in 1868 and functioned until 1894 when Stretford Urban District Council became responsible for the running of Stretford and Trafford Bar. By 1933 the area had developed a great deal and the great industrial area known as 'Trafford Park' had been added. Around 60,000 people lived in the 3,000-plus acres that came under the control of Stretford Borough Council. It is the region that in 1933 was known as Stretford that we show in this book. The names Old Trafford and Stretford are known the world over because of sporting connections: the late, great John Arlott spread our fame further every time he said: 'And now, here at Old Trafford, we start another Test Match, bowling from the Stretford end.'

THE STREETS
OF STRETFORD

In this section we take a look at the area that was the original Stretford. There was never a village centre as such, the parish developing within the triangle of streets now known as Barton Road, Chester Road and Kingsway. Barton Road was formerly Higgin Lane, King Street was Gamershaw Lane, and part of Chester Road was known as Turnpike Road.

The shops on the north side of King Street, c. 1964. All the shops in the foreground have been demolished and the road built over. Some of the buildings at the top of the picture were incorporated within the Arndale shopping centre, which now provides the people of Stretford with a modern indoor shopping complex.

King Street, Stretford, c. 1968. Shopping may have taken longer in those days, going from shop to shop, but there was plenty of variety. These are a few of the shops along King Street pictured not long before they were all demolished to make way for the Arndale Centre.

The view across Chester Road from Dorset Street, looking into the entrance of the Longford Super Cinema and Café in July 1939. It was a splendid building in art deco style, and was very typical of the super cinemas that were springing up all over the country at that time. It had Venetian marble flooring in the entrance, special soundproofing and air conditioning, and two specially commissioned murals painted by F.H. Baines DA. The auditorium itself was decorated in tangerine and silver blue and the luxury seats had underseat heating! After the show you could wine and dine in the Café-Restaurant.

The site of an accident outside the Civic Theatre in Chester Road, Stretford, 29 July 1939. These two pictures were taken to show the scene of the accident and the state of the road but they also show the centre of Stretford at a time when Britain was facing up to the Second World War. Life would never be the same again. NO PARKING had been painted on the pavement outside the gents outfitters and also visible is the entrance to the Longford Cinema.

Chester Road, looking south towards Sale. The Civic Theatre is on the right. Edge Lane is officially the A34 to Cheadle while the B5213 is the road to Urmston. Next to the Civic Theatre is the Talbot Hotel, selling Openshaw Ales; outside the Civic Theatre are posters explaining 'black-out' procedures.

Chester Road, Stretford, c. 1958. This main road runs north to south through Stretford and thus dominates many photographs of the area. This part used to be called Turnpike Road. The two tall landmarks are St Ann's Church spire and the Civic Hall. Both have survived.

King Street, Stretford, 1967. This view is towards the library from the post office. Just visible on the left are the shops of Andrews, Jacksons and Ashcrofts jewellers. Work had already started on the Arndale Centre behind these shops.

The view up Edge Lane, photographed from King Street Corner at the junction of Edge Lane and Chester Road, *c.* 1962. William Deacon's bank on the corner is still there, with plenty of parking spaces in front of the shops.

Another view up Edge Lane towards Stretford station, with the bank on the corner, but this picture was taken much earlier than the one above. There is no sign of the Longford Super Cinema entrance, built beyond the block of shops in 1935.

Stretford, photographed from the top of Stretford House, 4 June 1969. St Matthew's Church is immediately below, and the first phase of the Arndale Centre is nearly complete. The new Kingsway was

not yet built, but the area was being cleared in readiness. Chester Road is still only two lanes, and some of the shops still await demolition, especially those at the post office end of King Street.

Another photograph taken from Stretford House, *c.* 1977. The dual carriageway has now been completed, sweeping away the bank and some of the shops on the corner of Edge Lane, and the remaining shops along this part of Chester Road. This view is very similar today.

Another view of Stretford, a little further to the right than the one above, but taken on the same day. The Drum public house is situated to the rear of the site of the Angel Hotel which was demolished to make way for the road widening. St Matthew's Church Hall is in the bottom left corner.

Chester Road, Stretford, photographed from the middle of the road outside the Civic Hall (Theatre), January 1938. The Hall is sometimes wrongly described as the Town Hall or Old Town Hall. It was used by the council as offices for a short time when the council acquired it in 1910 from Mrs Rylands' estate for £5,000, having rented it since John Rylands' death in 1893. John Rylands built the hall (to a design by Lofthouse) in 1878 to serve as the Assembly Rooms and Library for the people of Stretford, many of whom were employed on his estate. The old fire escape can be seen clearly on the left of the picture. The spire of St Ann's Church is visible on the skyline. Work began on this church in 1862 and it was built to a design by E.W. Pugin, who also designed the Presbytery adjoining. It is less ornate than Pugin's other church in the area, Barton monastery, but it certainly makes a graceful landmark along the main Chester Road. It was paid for by Sir Humphrey de Trafford and his wife Lady Annette, who owned much of the land in the Stretford area.

The Old Pinfold and the cottage behind, 1898. In Edwardian times this view became popular as a postcard picture and was given the title 'Old Stretford'. The pinfold was a place where stray animals were kept until their owners collected them and paid the fine for letting them stray.

Looking up King Street from Chester Road, *c.* 1900. The site on the right was later occupied by the Picturedrome and the post office. Opposite was Wakefield's Italian Warehouse which was a popular store. Note the beef hanging outside J. Riley's. The house on the right with the sign on the wall was Sherlock's Smithy.

Work in progress on widening Edge Lane, photographed for the *Stretford Journal* in the 1960s. The Bridgewater Canal runs along the bottom of the picture, and in the middle is the Talbot Hotel, which stood on the other side of Chester Road. Also visible is the Essoldo Cinema: its unusual name was said to be an amalgamation of the name of the cinema chain's owner and those of his wife and daughter. His wife was Es(mé), he was Sol(omon) and his daughter was Do(reen), hence Es-sol-do.

King Street, Stretford, 1960s. This shopping area was typical of any high street in the country. We all knew and loved the little shops, but looking at this picture it does look slightly run down, and Stretford was lucky – it became one of the first places in the country to have an Arndale Centre.

Wakefield's Corner, King Street, *c.* 1968. The Trafford Arms which originally stood here was demolished in 1863 and Wakefield's Italian warehouse was built on the site. After they moved out it became Gees, and Gees Corner still appears above the taxi sign; note also the LON telephone code for Longford. This picture must have been taken only weeks before demolition because the windows have 'Closed' and 'Closing Down' painted on them.

King Street, Stretford, *c.* 1890. At this time the street still had a residential feel to it. This picture was taken from the Chester Road end by local photographer Frank Hulme. The Conservative Club is on the right.

Chester Road, Stretford, photographed from the Civic Hall, *c.* 1898. Note the horse-drawn tram which ran from Manchester out to the 'Old Cock'. The area was still quite rural in those days, and was a popular retreat for rich merchants from Manchester who wanted to get away from the grime of the city.

Chester Road, again taken from the Civic Hall, early 1960s. There are still houses with gardens on the left but most of the houses on the right have been converted into shops over the years.

Chester Road, Stretford, 1968. This picture illustrates the variety of shops along this part of Chester Road. The building with the peaked roof in the centre of the picture was the Midland Bank; originally a Temperance Hotel, it was built, like so much else, by John Rylands, who was himself a teetotaller and did not like his workers to drink either.

The shops on Barton Road, *c.* 1951. The tree and the greenery are all that is left of the pinfold and Pinfold Cottage. Since this picture was taken the corner has been widened and developed, with more shops and Pinfold Court flats built a little way back from the corner.

The rear of 52 and 53 Barton Road, Stretford, just before demolition, *c.* 1930. Also visible is the thatched roof of 'The Fow't' which stood on Higgin Lane, the former name for Barton Road. These buildings were part of New Shed Farm.

This garage and repair shop stood at 33 Lostock Road, Barton. Its ramshackle appearance was unlikely to inspire confidence in its customers hoping for quality service. When Park Road was constructed to improve access to Trafford Park, Lostock Road became Barton Road, and this became no. 344.

Taylor's Square, *c.* 1916. The Square was behind Chester Road, around nos 1145–1159.

A rear view of the shops on Chester Road which backed on to Taylor's Square. Through the gap you can see the new post office buildings, built in the early 1930s shortly before the Square was cleared away.

Nos 1205 and 1207 Chester Road. Older properties were to be found down in the village area of Stretford. By 1920 most of them were in a rather dilapidated state. This picture was taken by the UDC just before most of the area was cleared. The spire in the background belongs to the Congregational Church, built in 1860 (not to be confused with St Ann's.)

The rear of 1209 Chester Road, *c.* 1929, showing the remains of what looks like a barn and an outside privy.

King Street and the corner of Bennett Street, 1929. The latter was named after 'Ready Money John Bennett', a Manchester councillor who built the houses in this area. This site is now occupied by the Stretford Library. The Methodist church is visible on the left.

Another view of King Street, but looking the other way, showing the shops on Bennett Street and King Street Corner where the Medical Centre is today.

King Street, Stretford, 1900. Originally called Gammershaw Lane, the name was changed to celebrate George II's accession to the throne. The Primitive Methodist chapel stood where Stretford Library stands today. This picture was sold in 1906 by A. Hargreaves, printer, of Edge Lane, Stretford. Printer he may have been, but it was still cheaper to have the cards printed in Saxony, as most small firms did between 1905 and 1910.

Rear view of 5–19 Pinnington Lane, 1934. Pinnington Lane is situated opposite the Kingsway entrance to the Arndale Centre. Few of the old 'Lane' names have survived. Note the sanitary block to the right for the older and narrower houses behind.

The Stretford Ees is an undeveloped area which is subject to regular flooding when the River Mersey rises. Flood gates behind the cemetery are used to take the pressure off the river by diverting the water into the Ees. 'Eye Platt' Bridge crosses this flood area. The river overflow channel runs under the Bridgewater Canal Aqueduct, shown here in 1936.

The Toll House at Crossford Bridge, *c.* 1878. The toll to cross into Cheshire was a half-penny for laden horses and mules and one penny for carts.

This picture of the bend in Barton Road (where Park Road joins it today) was taken by a motor-cycling enthusiast, *c.* 1930. This area had many old cottages, some with wooden porches over the front door similar to this one. Barton Road used to be called Coal Pit Lane and the former name for Park Road, before the opening of Trafford Park, was Butt Lane.

The Easiephit shop was part of the Picturedrome Building, photographed shortly before demolition in 1969. The notice in the window reads 'Business Transferred to Unit No. 5'.

The Easiephit shop, Greenlees & Sons, on King Street, 1968. It was demolished soon after to make way for the Arndale Centre but this picture shows business as usual, with windows full of stylish shoes, sandals and handbags. Meesons sweets and tobacco shop next door looks as if it had already closed down. The Picturedrome building, erected with such pride in around 1912, was Stretford's first purpose-built cinema, and shops were incorporated into the design. It was a distinctive building, with its unique tiled front. Unfortunately, although it was an important part of Stretford's social life, it was removed when Chester Road was widened; the underpass comes up here now. The Arndale Centre, one of the first of its kind, has been a great success, although its future when the new massive Trafford Shopping Complex opens is uncertain. Will the developers move in once again?

Chester Road, Stretford, 1860. This is one of the earliest pictures of Stretford. The Trafford Arms stood at the corner of Kings Street and Chester Road; at this time the landlord was Frances Worrall. The rural nature of Stretford is very apparent, with a flock of sheep being driven past J. Bray (painters) shop, despite its proximity to Manchester's grimy city centre. This early picture was reproduced as a postcard from 1905.

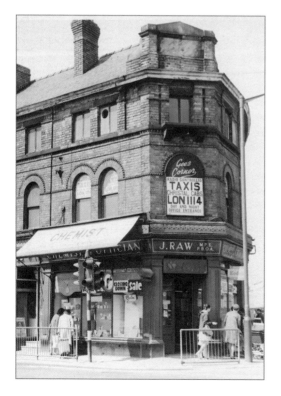

This photograph shows the same view as the above but almost a hundred years later. The building was originally Wakefield's Shop, a grocer's emporium, then later became Gee's Corner. Chemist J. Raw MPS, FBOA was the last occupant and they were having a closing down sale when this picture was taken in 1968.

The 'village' end of Chester Road, 1910. These cottages are numbered 1220 to 1228. The parish church of St Matthew's is behind. Today this part of Chester Road is very different.

Rear view of 1220–1228 Chester Road. The sign on the shed to the right reads: 'This Shed Must Not Be Broken Into'! I wonder if it worked?

Nos 346 and 348 Barton Road just before demolition. These old farm buildings have had their day, as Stretford had long since turned its back on farming, although what looks like rhubarb is growing in the field nearest the buildings, Stretford being famous for its rhubarb. As the population of Stretford grew, more land was needed for housing.

No. 9 Moss Road, again just prior to demolition. This was one of many derelict old cottages that were eventually pulled down to make way for new housing.

Kenwood Road, Stretford, *c*. 1920. John Rylands added more houses to the few already in existence: there were £50 'mansions' for middle-class managers, many of whom worked for him, and £20 terraces for working-class people. Parker Street became Cromwell Street (and later Cromwell Road), Steven Street became Norwood Road and Harriett Street became Kenwood Road. At the end of the road is a church built by John Rylands; this was renamed Rylands Hall when it was converted into business premises in 1985.

No. 348 Barton Road, *c*. 1910. This part of the road was formerly Higgin Lane, leading to Coal Pit Lane. These old cottages looked towards Urmston, still very rural at this time.

This painting depicts the Wheat Sheaf Hotel, built in 1760. Known locally as Bowker's Inn (and complete with a bowling green), it stood on the corner of Chester Road and Pool End Lane, a small curved street which ran between King Street and Chester Road. Pool End Lane became Market Street in about 1800 when Stretford's market started.

The junction of Barton Road, Chapel Lane and Sandy Lane, 1920s. Note the absence of traffic.

The rear of 1220–1228 Chester Road. Each house had a garden, a vegetable plot and out-buildings and of course an outside lavatory.

The lavatories, or 'water closet compartments', stood in the yard behind the houses. Heading down to the 'lavvy' with a candle and a copy of the *Daily Sketch* was the norm.

The view down Chester Road from roughly opposite Derbyshire Lane in the late 1950s. All the houses on the left were demolished and the road was widened into a dual carriageway in the 1970s.

The Old Police House in King Street, Stretford. The Stretford Police were part of the Lancashire Division, never Manchester Division. It is a matter of record that the first ever Lancashire policeman to be murdered was PC Nicholas Cock of Stretford (Old Trafford) Division. He was killed by the villainous Charlie Peace who lived in Chorlton, but who did much of his thieving in Stretford. This old house was replaced by the modern building on Talbot Road, between the Town Hall and the Technical College.

This is the original Catholic chapel in Herbert Street off Chester Road, pictured in the late 1970s. It was built and paid for very discreetly by the de Trafford family; they subsequently built St Ann's Church in 1862, the spire of which is visible in the background. This little chapel is now lost among the tightly packed housing and garages around it. The de Traffords, who did so much for the area, made donations towards churches of both denominations even though they themselves were staunch Roman Catholics. Stretford lost a great deal when the generous de Trafford family sold Trafford Park in 1896 and moved south. Even so, more than half of the ground rents in the Stretford UDC area was held by the de Traffords in 1930; indeed much of the land in the Stretford area is still owned by the family.

These combination cards from the early 1960s were published by Lilleywhite Ltd of Brighouse, Yorkshire. The top picture shows views of Chester Road, King Street, Edge Lane and the Town Hall, with St Matthew's parish church in the centre. The bottom picture is an odd combination, with four views of Victoria Park around the Town Hall, pictured from the Gardens, which were always beautifully laid out.

OLD TRAFFORD
& GORSE HILL

*Historically and geographically, Stretford and Old Trafford (Brooks's Bar) are unlikely partners —
they were combined as Stretford simply because the lords of the manor were the Trafford family. The
original Old Trafford area, and out to Brooks's Bar, always felt that it belonged more to
Manchester, and the local people did not venture often to the King Street end of Stretford,
preferring the bustling streets of Moss Side and Hulme.*

*The Trafford Road Swing Bridge in the 1960s. Trafford Park Road is to the left. You can just make out the
two wicker baskets on the bridge which were raised to signal right of way to shipping on the Manchester Ship
Canal which runs below the swing bridge. The signal on the lamp-post was used to give the tram drivers time
to put their brakes on when the bridge was about to be swung.*

Chester Road, Gorse Hill, *c.* 1908. The people lining the sides of the road seem to be waiting for something. Perhaps it was a motor car rally, as there are a number of cars all heading in the same direction.

The Old Cottages, Stretford, 1910, also known as Great Stone Cottages, Gorse Hill. Such postcards were sent all over the world: this one was sent by N. Hampson to Sam Bedford, at 22 Nightingale Street, Hamilton, Ontario. It cost one penny to send. How did it make its way back? Note Westinghouse water-tower in the distance.

An aerial view of Greatstone Road Secondary Boys' School, photographed soon after it opened in the 1960s. There are still a few houses in Chester Road at the bottom of the picture, but these were soon demolished to make way for the new sports centre built on the corner. Greatstone Road School was demolished in the early 1990s and the site is now occupied by PC World. The boys' school joined with Gorse Hill Girls' Secondary to form Stretford High School, using the grammar school buildings on Greatstone Road, while the boys from the grammar school joined the Girls' Grammar School on Edge Lane.

The view looking south along Chester Road towards the centre of Stretford, 17 June 1963. The photographer was standing on Longford Bridge, which crosses the Bridgewater Canal. The first bridge was built here in 1766 when the canal arrived. St Ann's Church dominates the skyline. Aldon Sport & Casual Wear were using the building on the right and the road coming in is Davyhulme Road East.

Photographed on the same day, this is Chester Road, Stretford, looking towards Gorse Hill. The photographer has passed Davyhulme Road East and turned to face Gorse Hill. The sign on the right informs us that the Forrest City Electrical Company have moved premises. The large building just beyond Longford Bridge on the left is the Stretford Electric Works, opened in October 1903 at a cost of £35,000. Behind this was the Gas Works.

The view from Greatstone Road railway bridge, looking down on the Government Buildings, mid-1970s. The Altrincham Electric Railway line is now used by Metrolink Trams. The low buildings on the far side are part of Lancashire cricket ground, and the back of the scoreboard is visible in the middle of the picture. The three buildings on the skyline were very distinctive: on the left is Alexander House, in the middle is Oakland House and on the right is the Lancashire Police Headquarters at Chester House on Boyer Street. The clock tower belonged to Norbury Printers on Elsinore Road. The Government Buildings were put up during the Second World War as an artificial limb centre where soldiers and other servicemen used to stay while they were fitted with artificial limbs and learned how to cope with their new life. The newsagent on Greatstone Road recalled how these men would be sent to his shop in the morning for a paper as a 'test' before they were allowed to return home. He was asked not to help them, even though some struggled up the one step into the shop. The buildings were later used for administration for the DHSS but were pulled down shortly after this picture was taken. There is now a housing estate on the site. The B&Q building, just out of the picture to the left, started life as a bowling alley which became the 'Hardrock' in the 1970s. Elton John, the Rolling Stones, Don MacLean and many other international stars appeared there.

The roundabout at the Quadrant, c. 1948. The Quadrant is the area where Kings Road and Greatstone Road meet. (The latter is named after the great stone which is now hidden in the bushes by Gorse Hill Park Gates.) The metal railings were removed for the war effort, and the iron seats have not yet been replaced. The shops provided everything the local community needed, and the Quadrant public house was very popular, not only with locals but also with visitors to the nearby cricket and football ground. These gardens, now called the Cliff Cronshaw Gardens, have been drastically remodelled; sadly, all the lovely cherry trees that ran through the centre have been cut down.

A closer look at the shops on the Quadrant, showing just how self-sufficient the area was. The shops included Bill the Butcher, a hardware shop, a chemist, a post office and a newsagent, as well as Martyn's Confectioners who were famous for their cream cakes. Eileen Roger's ladies haberdashery is now a bookmakers.

This is Trafford Bar in 1929, looking south towards Stretford. Chester Road leads off to the right with Talbot Road to the left. Talbot Road was named after Lady Mary Annette Talbot, sister of the Earl of Shrewsbury, who married Humphrey de Trafford in the first major public Catholic wedding in England since the Emancipation Act allowed freedom of worship to all. Harris's fish, fruit and flower shop stood on the right, and the newsagents next door has adverts for Players Navy Cut, Tournament Cigarettes 1s for 20, and Chairman Juniors only 4d for 10. Burgons Grocers stands between the two roads. The building has an eastern look, and the white elephant was a symbol of the brand of tea they sold. Further over to the left is Trafford Bar station, used today by the Metrolink. On the left, the bank is the white building among the houses. Both trams are on the number 27 route between Piccadilly and Trafford Bar, which terminated here.

Henrietta Street, Old Trafford, *c.* 1905. This was named after Sir Humphrey de Trafford's sister. The road was built about a century ago and the houses that faced Hullard Park had a very pleasant outlook. Note the cobbles and the lack of traffic.

Henrietta Street almost twenty years later. Both these postcards are from the J.L. Brown Series; they were a local firm who sold their images through the local shops. Hullard Park is on the left and just visible on the corner is the emergency callbox for police and fire calls.

Ayres Road, Old Trafford, *c.* 1910. The houses in this area were built for the better-off working class and the newly emerging middle classes who could afford to move out to the suburbs where the housing was better and conditions were much cleaner and brighter. There was, of course, excellent public transport in those days, with the train service at Old Trafford and the trams along the main roads, all taking the commuters to work in Manchester city centre, where the cotton manufacturers were thriving. In the distance is the square tower of St John's Church, which was built in 1904 to serve this burgeoning community.

Another view of Ayres Road from the junction of Northumberland Road, with Seymour Park School on the left, 1950s. It looks very peaceful. The church spire in the distance is St Mary's in Hulme.

Another J.L. Brown postcard, this is Stamford Street, Old Trafford, looking clean, neat and prosperous in the early 1920s. The two streets at this end of Ayres Road were named after the Earl of Shrewsbury and the Earl of Stamford, who both had connections with the de Traffords who owned all the land in this area. These houses were built in the late nineteenth century for the up and coming middle class who worked in Manchester city centre. The large houses, some of them four storeys, and the tree-lined streets made an attractive place to live. Stamford Street and Shrewsbury Street each had its own row of shops, including a haberdasher's, chemist's, baker's and grocer's, while Stamford Street also had a Co-operative store on the corner.

Seymour Park School, on Northumberland Road, described here as an Elementary School, in the early 1930s. This school was built to serve the increasing local population as more and more suburban mansions were built in the area. In its day it was ultra-modern with large airy classrooms, central heating and large playgrounds, just what the parents wanted for their children.

Seymour Grove, Old Trafford, 1903. This card was sent on Christmas Eve 1904 to Miss Williams of Fairlawn, Seymour Grove, to wish her Happy Christmas. The shops at the Trafford Bar end are still there today, but have changed to suit modern trends and now include the Wing Lee Chinese take-away.

An aerial view of the Royal Residential School for the Deaf (outlined) that stood between Chester Road and Talbot Road, 1920s. The school consisted of several large buildings. Chester Road is the wide road at the top of the picture, and Talbot Road is on the other side of the buildings lower down, with Boyer Street running between the two. The site of Henshaw's Blind Asylum, just outside the white lines facing Boyer Street, is now occupied by Lancashire Police Headquarters. Opened in 1837 the numbers of residents at Henshaw's increased steadily from 37 in 1839 to 161 by 1889. By the 1920s Henshaw's was turning out pupils 'taught and equipped to deal with life in the world at large' at the rate of nearly 200 per year. The White City Greyhound track has yet to be built, but you can see the railway lines ducking under Old Trafford to head out to Chorlton and all points south. (Photo: N.S. Roberts)

Seymour Grove, Old Trafford, *c.* 1908. Taken from the Trafford Bar end, this picture gives some impression of the large houses that stood along this road. The cobbled road on the right is Tennis Street, so named because originally it led down to the Manchester Tennis Playing Grounds. The tennis courts have long gone, but the name Tennis Street remains.

The more modest houses in Seymour Grove, built between the wars, pictured in the 1950s. Seymour Grove was apparently named after Thomas Seymour, the founder of T. Seymour Meads the grocers, who, after making his money, donated land to create Seymour Park nearby.

The Technical Institute on Stretford Road, Old Trafford, 1905. This 'seat of learning' was built here in an effort to stop people living in the Old Trafford (top) part of Stretford from complaining that too much was going on in 'the village'. The institute also served as a library for a time, and has been used for various educational purposes over the years. It is now the Fo Kuang Shan Buddhist Temple.

The caption on this photograph in a brochure printed sixty years ago describes this building as the Council Office, although it was really built as Stretford's Town Hall in 1887. This central site was chosen because it was deemed fairer to both 'ends' of Stretford. The lighter brickwork at the back of the building indicates the extension added in about 1908. Children of the 1950s knew this place as 'The Clinic' and for them it was quite an intimidating place. Today it is Trafford Hall Hotel, with a rather happier image.

Chester Road, looking towards Manchester, December 1937. Throstles Nest is behind the houses on the left. There had been an accident here and these two photographs were taken to show the state of the road. Thomas Goadsby, the former Mayor of Manchester, once lived in one of the large houses on the left of this picture, as did Abel Heywood later. The backs of these houses sloped down to the river (before it was turned into the Manchester Ship Canal), and in those days there were probably plenty of 'throstles' about (throstle is the old Lancashire name for a thrush).

Chester Road again, looking the other way. The policeman is on duty at the junction with Trafford Road, coming in from Salford. The waste area behind the hoarding on the right was used as parking for buses on 'football or cricket specials' or just waiting for the Trafford Park rush hour. All this area is now disappearing under another load of tarmac, and a new roundabout is being built.

Trafford Place, Old Trafford, *c.* 1900. This area has not been well documented in local history books, and pictures of it are scarce. Fishers Farm, the white building in the centre of the picture, stood on Fishers Street, and the terraced houses are in Trafford Place, off Johnson Street, behind the former Snooker Hall on Stretford Road. The photographer was standing at the side of the Wesleyan School, which belonged to the Wesleyan church which stood on City Road. This church later became St Brendan's and eventually St Lawrence's. The church, the school and the houses in this photograph have all gone: only the brick wall on the right and the building behind have survived.

Stretford Road, Old Trafford, looking towards All Saints', Manchester, October 1964. On the right is the Talbot Hotel (now closed) with the Platford adjoining it. The large building behind is the Luxor Club, formerly the Luxor Cinema, on Erskine Street (inside the Manchester boundary). The newly built flats on the left stood between White Street (now Trent Close) and Lucy Street, but were not yet occupied. The furthest block of flats now bears the name Rylands Court. Soon after this picture was taken Stretford Road was cut off by the construction of a dual-carriageway when they started the redevelopment of Hulme. It has since cost millions of pounds to restore.

Stretford Road, Old Trafford, looking towards Trafford Bar, 20 October 1964. The photographer was standing in the middle of the road in front of the Platford and Talbot Hotels. Lucy Street is just out of the picture to the right. The extensive demolition of this area was just beginning. A new housing estate has replaced the rows of older terraced houses on the left. The shops on the right have also gone to make way for more housing.

Chorlton Road, Brooks's Bar, Old Trafford, 1920s. This view was taken from outside the Whalley Hotel looking up Chorlton Road. Moss Lane West is on the right and Upper Chorlton Road is off the picture to the left. The bank on the corner of Moss Lane West is now a betting office. Bates' post office is now a solicitors' office. The spire in the distance belongs to the Congregational church, most of which was demolished in 1972.

The view down Upper Chorlton Road, Brooks's Bar, 1905. The Stretford border runs down the centre of the road, so that everything on the right side of the photograph is in Stretford, and everything on the left in Manchester. The church, which stands on the corner of Stamford Street, was saved from certain demolition by the large community of West Indian people living in the area, who bought it and renamed it the New Testament Church of God. Only the top part of the tower has been removed.

CIVIC PRIDE

On 16 September 1933, a very important day in Stretford's history, the title Urban District of Stretford passed into history, as had the Stretford Local Board in 1894. The new Stretford Borough showed that it was up to the Royal Charter of Incorporation given that day. Perhaps 16 September should be 'Stretford Day', with special events to celebrate it every year.

The great day started with the Mayor, Councillor Sir Thomas Robinson OBE, leading the councillors in procession from the Civic Hall to the new Town Hall on Talbot Road. The gentleman with the wig was the Town Clerk, Mr George H. Abrahams.

The huge procession arrived at the new Town Hall after walking from the Civic Hall on Chester Road. The weather kept fine as the dignitaries and invited guests held a service in front of the Town Hall steps. Children from local schools attended, and there was even a line of soldiers. It was a very important day for Stretford and was celebrated with due reverence.

Next the new Stretford Town Hall was officially declared open. The building was blessed and the children sang a hymn. Later the official party toured the new premises. In those days the leaders of local communities were invariably men who, having spent their lives as prosperous professional men, later in life felt it was their duty to give their time to the betterment of society by helping their own community. They took on these roles as a matter of honour, and received no financial payment, only the kudos of such positions. To our eyes they perhaps look somewhat archaic with their top hats and the Mayor and Town Clerk in their robes.

After the official opening of the new Town Hall, the celebrations continued in Longford Park, on the steps of Longford Hall. Here the official party is handing over the Charter of Incorporation. Naturally all the church leaders had a few words to say on this special day. The four at the top table are, from left to right: Clr Frederick W. Bates MA, Deputy Mayor; Sir T. Robinson, Mayor; Lord Derby; and the Town Clerk, George Abrahams. The gentleman interested in his programme on the left of the table is Sir Humphrey Edmund de Trafford, the thirtieth Lord of Trafford and fourth Baronet. The family had already left Trafford Park and moved to London by the time he was born in 1891. It is nice to see him here and of course he would have been an honoured guest at these proceedings.

Alderman Albert Smith (right) presents Fred Bates, the Deputy Mayor, with the mace for the new borough. Made of silver gilt and 4 ft 3 in long, it weighs 155 oz. Alderman Smith had bought it as a gift for Stretford.

Every school in the area was represented on Charter Day, 16 September 1933. These photographs show the children waiting patiently in their groups on either side of the official platform. The weather was obviously good as the children are not wearing coats, and they looked very smart in their school uniforms, which included hats for the girls.

Many photographs were taken to record Stretford's Charter Day, 16 September 1933. This one shows the boys from Stretford Grammar School in the procession, wearing their red sports coats and red and black caps. As you can see, the day had quite a carnival atmosphere.

Alderman Fred Bates' portrait beaming down on the first floor Council Chamber in the Town Hall. This is one of six postcards specially made for the occasion by Mr A. Harold Clarke, photographer, of 83 Clarence Road, Chorlton-cum-Hardy.

The Committee Room on the first floor of the Town Hall. This large room could be divided into three by panels that were pulled across as necessary. The furniture was commissioned from Waring & Gillow and made at their Lancaster factory. The doors and panelling are of oak.

The main entrance of the Town Hall, 1933. The first sod was cut on 21 August 1931, and the building was designed by Messrs Bradshaw, Gass & Hope. An Ashton-under-Lyne firm, Edwin Marshall & Sons Ltd, were contracted to build it, and they used soft-tone wire-cut Ruabon bricks and pink stone from Darley Dale for dressing. The tower is 108 ft high.

Stretford Town Hall, *c.* 1970. Most of the space at the rear of the building is now covered by the Town Hall Extension and the notorious 'bombproof' shelter below the lawns. The original plan was for a large public hall to seat 2,000 people, where shows and pantomimes as well as public meetings could be staged. Beyond the clock tower is the Lancashire County Cricket Ground and the four office blocks named after famous cricketers: Duckworth, Statham, Washbrook and McClaren.

Longford Hall was built by John Rylands and sold in 1910 to the people of Stretford by the executors of John Rylands' wife's will. Here we see the Hall shortly after the handing-over. It was used as an art gallery as well as for holding exhibitions and other public events. It was a handsome building, and lent dignity to many functions held there. Queen Elizabeth held a garden party on the lawns in front of the Hall in 1977 during her Jubilee celebrations.

Stretford Urban District Council used the large greenhouse/conservatory attached to Longford Hall to stage floral displays and people would come from all over Manchester to see them. 'You walk through the warm humid scented air, with smells that lingered all the way home,' said one visitor. This postcard shows a fine display of plants and greenery from the 1920s.

CELEBRATION OF THE CORONATION OF
KING GEORGE AND QUEEN MARY,
JUNE 22ND, 1911.

SOUVENIR TIN OF TEA.

PRESENTED WITH THE COMPLIMENTS AND
GOOD WISHES
OF THE
Stretford Urban District Council.

JOHN KELSALL, CHAIRMAN.

On the occasion of the coronation of King George IV and Queen Mary on 22 June 1911, Stretford Urban District Council gave each pensioner in the district a gift: men received a souvenir tin of tobacco and the ladies a souvenir tin of tea. One of these cards accompanied each gift.

Mabel Jones, Stretford's Pageant Queen, 13 July 1935. Her ladies in waiting include the retiring Queen, Patricia Collins, with her 'ladies', on Mabel's right. On her left is the Lancashire Cotton Queen, Miss E. Taylor. The Mayor Fred Bates and his wife, the Lady Mayoress, are next to the queens. Also present are the Pageant Chairman, H. Lord, and his wife.

Town Hall, Chester Road, Stretford - 1898.

A horse-drawn open-topped tram passing the Talbot Hotel, on Chester Road, *c.* 1898. The Talbot Hotel was built in around 1870, replacing the older Bishop Blaize inn which had stood on this spot for centuries and was demolished in 1863. Next to the Talbot Hotel is the Civic Hall, which the caption erroneously calls the Town Hall; just to confuse things it is now officially called Stretford Public Hall.

Miss Gladys Boyling, Stretford's Rose Queen, 1910. Stretford Pageant began in around 1909, when it was decided that the Rose Queen should walk in procession from Stretford to Gorse Hill Park. It became an annual event and continued until the First World War intervened. After the war, as part of the effort to raise morale, it was decided to make the Pageant as big as possible, and to switch to Longford Park for the ceremony. The first real Stretford Pageant as we know it was held in 1919.

The new pool and extension at Cyprus Street Baths, Stretford, photographed on its opening day, 10 May 1913. When John Rylands died in 1888 the good work he had set in motion did not stop, his wife, Enriqueta, continuing that work with added zeal. When she died in 1908, her executors ensured that money was made available to finish her various enterprises, including this extension to the Baths her husband had given in 1885.

A crowd gathers to watch the opening of the new Public Baths in Cyprus Street, 1913. In the background is a sign for Ivy Cottage Dairy, advertising 'warm milk, delivered twice daily' and new-laid eggs.

The official party at the opening ceremony inside the baths, which were declared open at 3 p.m. by Councillor Herbert Lewtas, Chairman of the Town Hall and Baths Committee, assisted by John Whiteside, Chairman of the Council. The baths were bombed in 1940, but were repaired and reopened; they survived until the 1970s.

The staff of Stretford Library in the brand new Central Library building which opened on 26 November 1940. Seated at the front is Mr Threlfall, the Chief Librarian. On his right is Miss Carline, the Children's Librarian, who held a 'Story Hour' every Saturday morning in the 'study'. The Stamp Club and the Meccano Club also met there. The Children's Library was damaged by a bomb soon after it was opened, and moved up into the Art Gallery 'for the duration'.

Stretford High School for Girls, off Chester Road, c. 1920. The building on the right, Heath House, started life as an orphanage, before becoming integrated with the newer buildings on the left. The girls were evacuated to Macclesfield at the outbreak of the war, but had moved back when the school was hit by a bomb in 1940. The school was never rebuilt on this site, becoming instead Stretford Girls' Grammar School on Edge Lane.

Old Trafford Senior Boys' School on Stretford Road was opened officially on Saturday 4 January 1930 by Councillor A. Smith. This was part of Stretford UDC's campaign to 'look after the "Old Trafford" end'. It is now Old Trafford Junior School but it is soon to be pulled down.

Assembly Hall at Old Trafford Senior Boys' School, 4 January 1930. 'Guests will assemble at 2.45 p.m. at the school forecourt. The Architect Mr Percy Howard ARIBA will present a medallion to Councillor A. Smith who will open the School. The Guests will then proceed to the Assembly Hall for the remainder of the Proceedings.'

Officials at the ceremony held to mark the relocation of the Trafford Estate entrance gates and lodges to their new position at the entrance to Gorse Hill Park in Chester Road, *c.* 1928. The Park was opened in about 1900 as Gorse Park on land that was formerly Gausehill Farm. When the cenotaph was erected on Chester Road the council decided to move the Trafford Gates and make the whole area grander.

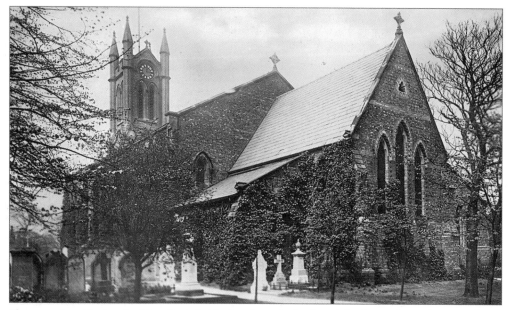

The present parish church of Stretford, St Matthew's was built of stock brick to a design by W. Hayley in 1842. It was one of the Commissioners' Churches and cost £2,700 to build. The foundation stone was laid by Lady Laura Anne Trafford on 30 September 1841. The church was dedicated by the Bishop of Chester on 10 October 1842. Unfortunately this day clashed with a horse-racing meeting on Stretford Ees, and Sir Thomas Joseph de Trafford (who had obtained royal permission to use the 'de' in October 1841) only stayed for a moment before going on to the races.

All Saints' Church, Stretford, was built on the corner of Cyprus Street and School Road. The foundation stone was laid on All Saints' Day in 1884 and it was officially opened on 20 November 1885. This picture shows the church after it was enlarged in 1906. There was a Sunday School to the rear, which became a Day School as more people moved into the area. The church was another victim of the war, and was rebuilt on Barton Road, by the railway bridge; it was the first church in the Manchester Diocese to be rebuilt after the war.

St Bride's Church, Shrewsbury Street, Old Trafford, August 1973, just before it was demolished. A new smaller church now stands on this spot. The steelwork is now the Library and Community Centre. Work began on the church in 1878, to a design by Pennington & Brigden and it took six years to complete. The Rectory, which still stands, was built in 1880. In 1891 two members of Col. Cody's 'Wild West Troop' were married here and the register has the 'marks' of the groom 'Black Heart' and his wife 'Calls the Name', sister of 'No Neck'. L.S. Lowry was baptized in this church.

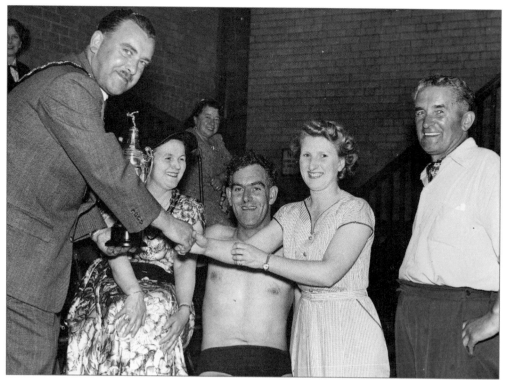

The Mayor of Stretford, Councillor Maxted, presents the Borough Trophy for Stretford Amateur Swimming Club in the 1955/6 season. Mrs Maxted is next to him, with Doug Francis in the middle; Mrs E. Nancollas is shaking hands with the mayor, while Mr J. McPherson looks on.

The Arms of the Borough of Stretford, granted in 1935 and defunct when Trafford took over on 1 April 1974. 'Service and Efficiency' was the motto. The hand with the thunderbolt represented Industry and was adopted by Atlas Lamps, made by Westinghouse, in Trafford Park. The roses represent Lancashire and the flail and scythe for the de Traffords. (The family adopted these emblems in honour of one of their ancestors who, according to legend, hid his treasure under some straw and pretended to be a simpleton thrashing the straw when Government forces came to relieve him of his fortune.) The lion stands for John of Gaunt, and the ship at the bottom represents the links with the rivers Mersey and Irwell. Previously, Stretford UDC had a badge of three lions, the top one with a bar, and this symbol can still be seen on Victoria Park Gates and Gorse Hill School on Burleigh Street.

PARKS & RECREATION

The very first open space provided for the village of Stretford was an area around Henshaw Street, near Victoria Park Junior School. The recreation grounds, known as the 'Rec', came into being in about 1890 with separate playgrounds for boys and girls. It had the usual things: swings, slides, parallel bars and even a trapeze for the boys. The cinder area was used for open air meetings and choral singing.

The 'Rec' was replaced around the turn of the century by a more formal area, Victoria Park, shown here on an early postcard from about 1905. The Westinghouse Tower on the skyline indicates the proximity of Trafford Park.

When Queen Victoria died, all of England set about building monuments and parks in her honour. Stretford was no exception, creating Victoria Park, its first formal park. The stretch of Pinnington Lane which ran alongside the Park had its name changed to Victoria Road. These gates are still standing today, and the plaques on the side read 'These gates were presented to the Township of Stretford by John Slyman, November 15th 1902'. The plaque on the right reads 'To Perpetuate the Memory and Beneficial Reign of Her Most Gracious Majesty Queen Victoria'. John Slyman, Chairman of Stretford UDC, was a vicar's son who lived for many years at Thorncliffe, 112 Urmston Lane. He was a teacher by profession and was Superintendent of the Sunday School at St Matthew's Church.

Victoria Park, 1920s. It was the pride of Stretford UDC, with its neat and well-tended gardens. On the park gates is the badge of the three lions, the emblem that Stretford had adopted.

A charming study of a mother and daughter strolling through the gardens, c. 1925. The park covered 19 acres and boasted several good bowling greens, a children's play area, and beautifully laid out formal gardens.

Hullard Park, Old Trafford, 1922. This park was opened by Stretford UDC early this century. It was only a small park, just over 11 acres, but it was well equipped with a lovely Victorian bandstand, several bowling greens, a croquet lawn, an alpine rockery and a Veterans' Club. The caption on the card has wrongly described Old Trafford as Manchester.

Hullard Park, c. 1910. The park was formed from land belonging to Hullard Farm. Older maps refer to the farm as Hullard Hall; it was not unusual for larger farms to take the title 'Hall'. The farmhouse itself survived until 1912 when it was pulled down to make way for new housing. The streets around the park — Fulford, Thorpe and Walter Streets — were laid out on the site of the farm and its out-buildings.

Longford Hall and Gardens have been a controversial topic in Stretford for over a hundred years. In this 1938 aerial view the Hall is in the centre with its conservatory. The gardens on the right had their own greenhouses, a café, and shelters on either side where you could sit if the weather wasn't too good. In the far distance on the right is Firswood. This area did not belong to the Trafford family. Originally it was owned by the Mosley family, Lords of Manchester, who owned land in Longford, Derbyshire, and thus called this Longford Farm. It was given in around 1693 to John Bland when he married Lady Ann Mosley, but he mortgaged the land off. Later the very powerful Powell family divided up the land, separating and developing the Chorlton end; they also began to divide Turf Moss. Longford Farm was subsequently sold for £4,600 to Parker Raingill, a rich pork butcher from Stretford. He built Beech House, the first house on Edge Lane, with barns, shippons, stables and a slaughter-house behind. He created three streets, Parker Street, Steven Street, and Harriett Street, the last two named after his son and wife respectively. Parker rented out the farm and then it was bought by Thomas Walker, a Manchester Boroughreeve, as a 'retired gentleman's retreat'. Walker laid out gardens and lawns which became the basis for Longford Park. He was a great benefactor to the area, and when he died in February 1817 he was buried in St Clement's churchyard, Chorlton. John Rylands bought the estate in 1855 and lived at the old farmhouse while Longford Hall was being built; he lived in the Hall from 1857 until his death in 1888.

Longford Park Lodge Gates, 1910. The caption on this postcard says Chorlton-cum-Hardy, but the border is 200 yards further down Edge Lane (although some 20 acres of the park's 80 acres are in Chorlton). John Rylands built this lodge in about 1860, and it is still there today, but a bit dilapidated.

When John Rylands died in 1888 his third wife Enriqueta carried on his good works. She allowed the Hall and grounds to be used for civic occasions and charity fund-raising. The Zion Institute in Hulme is one of many organizations which benefited from her generosity. This postcard from 1909 illustrates one such grand social occasion.

Longford Hall, 1951. The gardens and the conservatory are still in good condition. The photographer is standing on the site of the original Longford farmhouse, where John Rylands lived while Longford Hall was being built, after which the farmhouse was pulled down and gardens created on the site.

Longford Hall Gardens, 1933. These beautifully laid out rose gardens were a credit to the gardeners who tended them. All the plants were grown in the huge greenhouses in the park, which also supplied plants for the Town Hall and Civic Hall, and for any public occasions. Many of the gardeners lived in the houses in the park and regarded their work as more than just a job.

The Fountain and Pond in Longford Park, Stretford, 1916. The Hall was bought 'for the people' in 1911 after a referendum was held in which the residents agreed to a raise in the rates of 2*d* to purchase the Park and Hall. During the First World War the Hall was used as a recuperation hospital run by the Red Cross. This card was sent from a soldier there to his friend back at camp; some of his message was crossed out in heavy black crayon before the censor passed and signed it.

Longford Hall, Longford Park, late 1970s. This is how most of us remember the Hall. It was a very handsome building, both inside and out. It was used by many organizations in the area for their various functions. There were many wedding receptions, as well as more formal occasions connected with the Borough. Stretford people were very proud of Longford Hall and it was shown off to visitors as the local stately home.

The care and neglect of Longford Park: this picture says it all! What a great shame the hall was left to rot and fall down. The gardens were in their prime, with mature trees and hedges. The lawns were perfect, and the flower beds a joy to behold, whatever the season. But the Hall was abandoned from 1983 until it was finally demolished in 1994 after much controversy. Now, in its place, is a formal garden that was opened, in a very low-key manner, at Easter 1997. It is sad that John Rylands, a man who is looked up to all over the world, is not commemorated in the area to which he gave so much. Even the chapel on Edge Lane, built and paid for by John Rylands and presently called Rylands Hall, is up for sale and its name may be changed by the new owner. (Photo: Keith Renwick)

The flower beds in the Royal Botanical Gardens. The Gardens opened in 1831 and had a fair measure of success. They were situated between Chester Road and Talbot Road. In 1857 Prince Albert himself helped to organize a 'United Kingdom Art Treasures Exhibition' and he opened the great collection, gathered from the houses and museums of the Empire, on 5 May 1857. The exhibition ran for 142 days and was visited by 1,336,715 people. Queen Victoria and most European royal families graced this affair, which gave the Gardens their royal prefix.

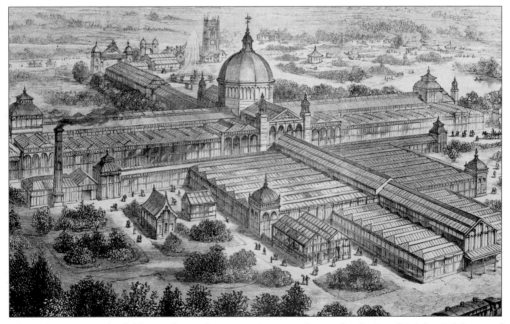

After a few years in the doldrums the gardens were chosen as the site for the Royal Jubilee Exhibition of 1887. The site had to be enlarged to take in all the exhibition halls shown here; the church was part of a 'Replica Manchester' built for the exhibition. It was a great success and ran for over six months. It was visited by nearly 5,000,000 people and it is recorded that on one bank holiday alone 75,000 people came to see it. It made a profit of £43,239 which was distributed to good causes in the area. The buildings were designed by Maxwell & Tuke, the firm that went on to design Blackpool Tower.

The Great Slide, White City, 1907. By the late Victorian period the Botanical Gardens had lost their attraction, and even though the management tried hard with an 'American Exhibition' in 1892, and various musical festivals and band concerts, the Gardens were in a very sorry state. In 1907 the site was sold and turned into a fun fair called White City. Many of the old buildings were given a lick of paint and a cosmetic face-lift and pressed into service.

White City, 1909. The former Industrial Hall is now the 'Fun Factory'. There were also river caves and a water chute. The cost of maintaining the amusements was high and because it had been put together 'on the cheap' it needed constant attention. Despite the management's best efforts the fun fair had closed within a few years. However, the buildings remained, and were left to rust and decay for several years. During the First World War the Manchester 'Pals' were billeted there, and in the 1926 General Strike, soldiers protecting strike-breakers were stationed there. The buildings were finally cleared in the late 1920s and White City Dog Track took over the site.

Old Trafford and White City, *c*. 1935. Part of the Botanical Gardens was now the White City Greyhound Racing Track. Chester Road runs along the top with Trafford Road just disappearing on the right. Talbot Road runs along the bottom left. Henshaw's Asylum and the Deaf & Dumb School are at bottom right and between them is the chapel, which was complete with its own minister and burial ground. One wonders whether the bodies were removed when they built the new Police Headquarters. The gates of White City, which started life as the Royal Botanical Gardens Gates, can be clearly seen on Chester Road.

SECTION FIVE

SPORT

Having two world-class sporting arenas in one small area is overpowering. The fact that they are both called Old Trafford – which happens to be the name of an area a few miles away – is even more confusing, but that is what we have in Stretford. Old Trafford is the home of Manchester United FC while Old Trafford is also the name of the Lancashire Cricket Club ground. They moved there when Prince Albert was arranging his Royal Art Exhibition in 1857 and took over the Clifford Cricket Ground.

Old Trafford football stadium was built in 1909 and opened on 19 February 1910. The first match was against Liverpool who spoilt the party by winning 4–3 in front of 45,000 spectators. John Davis had donated the £60,000 needed to build the new stadium. This photograph shows a Reserves match in progress in 1922; note how sparse the crowd is, and how open the ground.

Old Trafford, 1932. At bottom left is the Lancashire Cricket Ground – the covers are on, so it must be summer time! Beyond work is in progress on Stretford Town Hall. Its foundations were laid in 1931 and it opened in 1933. White City Greyhound Track is on the right with Old Trafford football ground at top left. This picture also shows the docks at Salford: the warehouses and the grain elevator on number 9 dock can be clearly seen. Notice the number of trees among the large houses on Talbot Road, and the large back-to-back houses where the Norweb (United Utilities) building is today. These roads were named Royal, Kings, Princes, and Queens as a reminder of the Royal Botanical Exhibitions. The Altrincham electric railway runs across the bottom of the picture. By this time there was a permanent station at Warwick Road, though temporary stations had been provided for both exhibitions.

Manchester United football ground, 1969. This postcard shows the rebuilt ground (it had suffered damage in the war) with the new floodlights in place. The recreation ground of Glover's Sports and Social Club is behind it. This pitch was also used for reserve games in the 1930s when visiting southern teams brought their second teams. The open end of the ground, the score-board end, is still remembered by thousands of older fans. Notice the railway station beside the ground, with a three-unit, six-coach DMU at the platform. The small local train ran from Central station and Piccadilly right to the ground, and returned after the match. This station brought thousands of supporters right to the ground, with very little trouble, but it is no longer used for Manchester United games. Recently it has also been used to bring in supporters for rugby league matches, and even visitors to a Christian concert held there.

The Manchester United team that played in the FA Cup Final on 4 May 1957. They lost to Aston Villa 2–1. Back row, left to right: Tom Curry (trainer), Duncan Edwards, Mark Jones, Ray Wood, Bobby Charlton, Bill Foulkes, Matt Busby. Front row: John Berry, Bill Whelan, Roger Byrne, David Pegg and Eddie Coleman. The missing player is Tommy Taylor who had caught a cold on the Saturday and was in bed with the flu when this picture was taken on the following Tuesday. The local newspapers could not afford to send a photographer to London for the match, so the team turned out for them on Hough End Playing fields.

Sir Matthew Busby CBE, the man who made Manchester United, pictured in 1947. Born in Scotland on 26 May 1909, he first came to England to manage Manchester City. Thousands lined the streets of Stretford as this papal knight and Freeman of Manchester made his final journey to the church he always attended in Chorlton (*see* page 125).

The staff of Manchester United, 1960s. How many famous faces can you spot in the Reserve and A Teams?
Many of them are now household names, known throughout the world. Indeed, fans come from all over
the world to the United Ground, not only to see their heroes play but also to see the museum and shop
where souvenirs are big business: it's all part of modern football.

George Best. He made his United debut
against West Brom. on 14 September 1963. In
spite of his rip-roaring reputation, George
Best always thrilled the fans when he played,
and became a footballing legend. He played
the last of his 361 games for Manchester
United on New Year's Day 1974. As with
many of the colourful characters who appear
in various walks of life from time to time,
George Best has become the possession of the
media, and he can still make headlines
whatever he does.

Stretford Nomads AFC with their trainer and manager, 1911–12. This picture was taken a year after Manchester United had arrived in Stretford. Here the Nomads are showing off the Manchester Union League Cup they had just won, along with the Chorlton and District League Cup. They were getting off to a promising start.

The Old Cock football club posing on Turn Moss, c. 1976. Many local amateur football teams play here; football is, after all, our national sport, and everyone wants to take part; and even if they don't make it to the professional realms, the standard of play in small amateur teams is excellent. That is why open areas are so important to local people. In the background is the 23-storey Stretford House with St Matthew's Church tower further to the right. Places like Turn Moss in Stretford are continually threatened by creeping urbanization.

Stretford Cricket Club's 1st Team, pictured at their Lesley Road ground before their last match of 1976. The match was against another local team, Sale Moor, who beat them by fifteen runs. Stretford has always had a very strong sporting tradition, kept alive by the fact that it has retained plenty of open spaces. At one time there were four different cricket grounds in the Old Trafford and Gorse Hill area, but over the years the pressure for land has reduced this number; nevertheless Stretford still has plenty of green areas left.

Cross-country running was compulsory at many schools and this picture shows Gorse Hill School boys running in Longford Park in 1951. The high wall in the background is where the animals are kept today, with the bowling green behind. These lads did not have fancy kit, just a coloured sash across their chests and pumps from Woollies. But they look as if they are giving it their all.

Gorse Hill School boys practising for the schools' Sports Day in White City, 31 May 1951. The Greyhound Stadium was regularly used by schools in the Stretford and Old Trafford area for their sports days. Today Stretford has much better facilities, notably the specially built sports stadium in Longford Park which hosts many top-class athletic meetings as well as events for local schools. Today White City is a retail park.

A photo finish at White City in 1951. The stadium is already run down: the stands have lost their roof and the whole place looks decidedly tatty. Before Stretford's new sports running track was built, would-be athletes had to use the White City track, as it was the only suitable venue. At night, of course, the track was used by the greyhounds.

PEOPLE & PLACES

Stretford Pageant in its heyday, 1935. Longford Hall in the background is bedecked with bunting, while the stage, the steps and the throne are pure theatre – and everybody loved it. Whatever part you played in this magnificent display you did with pride. It was all planned with clockwork precision by the pageant committee who controlled everything except the weather! This looks like a fine day.

Mabel Jones (*see* page 65) was elected Rose Queen in 1935. One of the first duties of the Rose Queen was to accept an official portrait of herself. Here Mabel receives her portrait from the Mayoress Mrs Bates while the Mayor and other civic dignitaries look on.

The 1976 Rose Queen with some of her retinue pictured during a visit to the local maternity hospital. Traditionally, the Rose Queen was expected to perform many civic duties throughout her 'reign'.

The Stretford Rose Festival was the forerunner of the Stretford Pageant of more recent times. This lovely Edwardian photograph was taken in Gorse Hill Park, where all the ceremonies took place, in around 1912.

Trafford Park had its own pageant, known as the Trafford Park Gala. This is Miss Margaret Brownlow, the retiring Gala Queen with her retinue in 1963.

The Stretford Children's Theatre was a well-known and much respected group. Here the founder Bertram H. Holland is presiding over a cast party in 1952. The young lady with the crown is June Ritchie, who shot to fame in 1962 in 'A Kind of Loving'. Several members of the Children's Theatre went on to become professionals in theatre, television and radio, notably Brian Trueman, David Duffy, Cynthia Sallabank and Stuart Simpson.

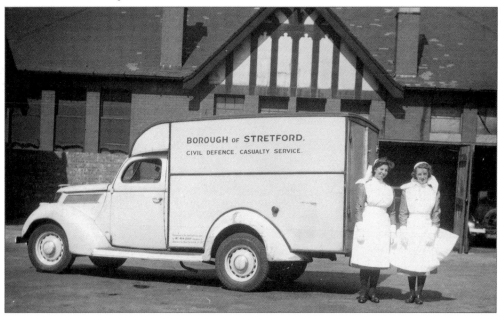

First Aid Post No. 2, complete with Civil Defence Casualty Service vehicle and a staff of two nurses at Seymour Park School in 1940. This area has a long history of looking after the injured in war time: during the First World War Lancashire County Cricket Ground building was turned into a hospital for soldiers (mostly American) and Longford Hall was used as a recuperation centre for gas and shellshock victims.

Her Majesty Queen Elizabeth II leaving Longford Hall and proceeding down the steps to a Royal Jubilee Garden Party held in Longford Park in June 1977. The Hall was a welcome stop for the Royal Party, and hundreds of people in Stretford turned out to welcome them.

Her Royal Highness Princess Anne, now the Princess Royal, visiting the Greater Manchester Police Headquarters, Chester House, Old Trafford, 5 June 1979. The building cost an estimated £4 million to build and boasted the most advanced technological telephone system. It was raining hard when the princess was greeted by Trafford's Mayor, Councillor Mike King, and the Chief Constable James Anderton.

Another famous visitor to Old Trafford was the first man in space, Yuri Gagarin, the Soviet cosmonaut, who was rocketed into orbit on 12 April 1961 aboard the *Vostock I* spacecraft. A year later, in 1962, he visited the Radar Establishment on Chorlton Road, to thank Decca Radar for their help in getting him down safely. From here he went on to Trafford Park to visit Metrovicks. As he toured through Stretford in his open-top car he was given a hero's welcome by the local people.

Staff at White City, *c.* 1910. At this time a bear pit with two brown bears was among the attractions listed.

Shop owners and their staff photographed outside their premises were a favourite subject for local street photographers, who would take orders for as many as fifty copies to be given to family and friends and even customers. This picture shows E.W. Midgley, family butchers, on Stretford Road, with Mr Midgley (second from left), his partner (left), their two assistants and the delivery boy (right).

Staff of L. Rocca's post office and newsagents, complete with uniforms, in the 1920s. That's L. Rocca herself in the middle. The post office is still in business today, and even the post box is in the same place. Dave and Pat Marsden run it today, keeping up the tradition of serving the community.

The staff of A. & D. Read, bakers and confectioners (formerly Whiteheads) of 1206 Chester Road, Stretford, 1950s. Again the staff have posed outside the shop.

Pupils from Gorse Hill Secondary School for Boys on Burleigh Road in Gorse Hill about to leave for their 'Whit Camp' in the Lake District in 1952. In 1958 the school moved from Burleigh Road to new premises at Greatstone Road School.

School photographs have been a source of embarrassment, humour and nostalgia since the words 'Come clean and tidy next Friday, we're having a school photo taken' were first uttered. This is class Standard II, Victoria Park Girls' School with their teacher in the early 1920s.

This is Class II at Gorse Hill Junior School in 1925. The boys were evidently expected to wear a tie for the occasion, whether it went with what they were wearing or not; doubtless they were whipped off as soon as the picture was taken.

St Matthew's Guides and Brownies taking part in the St George's Day Parade, 1960s. They are marching down Chester Road, before the road was widened and the shops demolished to make way for the new Arndale Centre.

St Matthew's Cubs taking part in the same Parade. These two pictures show the old uniforms: today they are quite different for boys as well as the girls.

King Street Primitive Methodist Sunday School Class, with their teacher Mrs Saunders, 1920. Back row, left to right: Harold Millar, Muriel Durden, Alfred Lamb, Harry Robinson, May Nicholson, -?-. Middle row: Hilda Wray, Lawrence Larter, ? Eckersley, Mrs Saunders, Ethel Hunt, ? Eckersley. The names of the three youngsters at the front were not recorded.

Cookery classes for the Women's Junior Air Corps (WJAC) under the eye of their CO, Miss Connie Mottram, 21 November 1942. 'Right, girls, take your dried egg powder and your substitute cream . . .' Connie is now Mrs Francis and is a stalwart of the Stretford Local History Society.

Volunteer nurses march proudly past the podium in front of Longford Hall on 17 May 1941. This was one of the events staged during 'War Weapons Week' to raise much-needed funds for the war effort. Lord Derby was among the dignitaries; he can be seen here with his walking stick, standing next to the Mayor of Stretford, Harry Lord.

Trafford Park Library was one of the 'village' amenities. The notice on the door reads 'The library will be permanently closed from 5th Sept. 1981'. Here we see Librarian Peggy Hutton locking up for the last time three weeks later; the books have gone, the fines have been collected and it's all over.

TRAFFORD PARK

Trafford Park has a fascinating and unique history. A private estate of a thousand acres or so, complete with all the trappings of a rich and powerful family, it went through many changes, not all industrial, and ended up as the world's first and largest industrial estate. Barnum & Bailey's Three-Ringed American Circus played in the Park for over six months. Manchester's first ever aerodrome was alongside Ashburton Road, where the famous aviator A.V. Roe made trial flights. Manchester Golf Club had a full-size eighteen-hole course here, and plans were even put forward for a horse-racing course to be sited here.

Trafford Hall, 1910. The fine square front of the hall, built in 1762, shows up well. The glass porch was added in about 1906 when the hall became a hotel and golf clubhouse. The back of the hall (on the left) was part of the old Wittleswick Hall. Trafford Hall was a large building with over 200 rooms. In 1763, when Hearth Tax was introduced, the Hall was recorded as having thirty-three hearths.

One of the few old buildings still standing in the Park today is the Trafford Park Hotel. This unusual view was taken from the bowling green at the side. This large hotel had plenty of room for residents as well as catering for local weddings and other celebratory functions. Today, the hotel is still prospering as well as being a stable feature in the changing face of the Park.

Looking at Trafford Park today it is hard to believe that it was once a place where people went for recreation. One of the main attractions was the large lake which was nearly a mile long. There was also an ice-house nearby. There was even a boat-building firm based on the lake. This is the boathouse where people could hire a boat for 6d per hour. (Photo: St Antony's Collection)

Trafford Park, *c.* 1912. At the bottom right is the Ford factory, and some of the houses built for the hundreds of workers who lived in the Park. Also visible is St Cuthbert's School and playground, and Third Avenue with the Trafford Park Hotel and bowling green at the junction with Ashburton Road. The lake can be seen at the top left, with the ship canal and Mode Wheel locks running across the top of the picture.

Westinghouse Works was the biggest in the Park: in 1910 it employed 10,000 men (and a few women in the offices). When American George Westinghouse agreed to build his factory here, the Park gained the first 'foreign' firm, which was run on American lines. A works police force and a strict no smoking policy were part of the tough regime. The factory produced trains for the London Underground, the Mersey Underground and the Liverpool Overhead Railway; ships' turbos; generators for Russia and Japan; Lancaster and Manchester bombers; and much more. The gas works in Gorse Hill can be seen at the top left.

Westinghouse Apprentice Training Room, 1914. If your father worked here he would get you in as an apprentice. Earlier, some of the management trainees had been sent to America to learn the 'company's ways' to make sure that their factories in Britain operated on the same lines as in America. Some of their innovations were a bit too advanced for the time, such as posi-drive screws and the three-pin plug, neither of which caught on and had to be dropped.

During the First World War the firms in Trafford Park played a vital role in the war effort. The men went to war and the women went to work. At one stage so many skilled men were enlisting that Westinghouse management had to go and ask for some of them to be brought back to teach the women how to do the jobs. The women had to do the work no matter how dirty or difficult, and were simply told where they had to report to for 'compulsory war work'.

War production at Westinghouse, 1916. Life was made more bearable for British and Russian troops fighting on the Russian Front by portable generators built here to fit the Russian railway gauge and shipped out to supply power and heat. This is 'D' aisle, the main production area.

Another young woman doing her bit in the First World War. She was one of thousands brought in to keep the factories producing the necessary goods to fight the war. They made shells, they operated machines and they worked the overhead cranes. The workplace had to alter to accommodate the female workers, and this vital work was one of the first steps in women's emancipation.

The Ford Company was one of many firms who took advantage of what the Trafford Park Estates Company had to offer, and set up business in 1911, taking over the premises of the British Electric Car Company. They brought over American workers who arrived on 21 October 1911 and within days the first Model Ts were rolling off the production lines. Relations between Ford and Trafford Park Estates blew hot and cold over the years, reaching a very low point in the 1920s; thus, when Ford got the chance of a new factory at Dagenham in 1931, they were off like a shot, using expansion as the excuse. They were tempted back for the duration of the Second World War for 'the country's good', building Rolls-Royce Merlin aircraft engines on a site in the corner of the park. Once again, many women took over the vital war work.

Trafford Park Road, *c.* 1928. This is the view towards the Trafford Road entrance to the Park. Glover's Cables was one of the first companies to come into the Park. This is a typical view of the Park, with workers either coming or going, some on their bikes, some on the bus, and a lot walking. The Park even had its own railway system to move goods to and from the factories.

W. & R. Jacob & Co.'s cream cracker and biscuit factory in Trafford Park, *c.* 1930. It is odd that among all the heavy industry and chemical plants, a food factory should spring up. This picture illustrates how well integrated and extensive the private railway system was. Most of the factories had their own line branching off the main system for easy access to and from their premises.

The Hovis grain elevator on the corner of Trafford Wharf Road and Elevator Road. Wheat and rye from the heart of Canada and America was transported across America, over the Atlantic and up the Ship Canal before finally being unloaded here. During the Second World War, this building was hit by an incendiary bomb and burst into flames. The fire raged for more than a week before they got it under control, but it continued to smoulder and flare up from time to time for another six months.

The view into the Park from the Trafford Road end of Trafford Park Road, 1916. This picture shows what a thriving area it was. Trafford Park had its own 'live-in' workforce, but thousands of people from the surrounding areas were also employed there. During the Second World War it was estimated that around 100,000 people worked in the Park, doing a huge variety of jobs from office workers to engineers, from biscuit makers to scientists. When the Park opened it had its own trams and later, buses, and was a remarkable example of industrial planning. Almost every factory was doing its bit towards the war effort: even Kilverts Lard Factory, its tower visible on the skyline, was turning out tons of grease for the shells, bullets and tanks made in the Park.

Trafford Park Public Prize Band, *c.* 1935. They are getting ready to play for the Sunday Parade at St Matthew's Church, Stretford. The village in the Park had everything it needed and was virtually self-contained. It had schools, churches, baths, a library and its own Prize Band. It has almost all gone now, and the people who lived there have been rehoused in the surrounding areas; all that is left of the old village is a hotel, a church, a row of shops, and St Antony's Heritage & Cultural Centre.

Whit Walks, *c.* 1936. The youngsters who lived in the close, strangely numbered streets used to hold their own Whit Walks; here, the Church of England scholars are seen in front of the Infant and Junior School, St Cuthbert's. The children are in lovely white dresses, some with knitted white bonnets.

Two of Trafford Park's youngest residents resplendent in their fancy dress costumes, *c*. 1963. They are pictured with two of the oldest residents during one of the last Galas held before the community was broken up and the people rehoused in other areas.

In 1980 plans were put forward to paint a mural on the end of this warehouse on Trafford Road, in tribute to the industry in Trafford Park. Walter Kershaw painted it on wooden sections and it was erected in 1982. After ten years work began on a more up-to-date version and this one was removed. The piece showing Denis Law celebrating a goal for Manchester United is now in St Antony's Heritage Centre on Third Avenue; it is signed by Denis Law and Walter Kershaw.

TRANSPORT

Stretford has never had its own bus or tram system. It always relied on Manchester or private companies such as the Cheshire Bus Co. and later the North Western Road Car Company of Crosville which had to pass through the area. The area has always been at the front of each transport revolution and has benefited from each one.

Trafford Park Estates had its own public transport system, which began with gas trams. When they began to struggle they were replaced by steam trains which turned out to be illegal, the public transport licence having been issued for single unit light trams, and so the Estate Company quickly brought in three AEC buses to bring in workers from Barton and White City. Here we see the three buses, open-topped and with solid tyres, waiting to go on duty just after their arrival in 1921.

The first real transport advance in Stretford was the arrival of the Duke of Bridgewater's Canal in around 1766. Its engineers James Brinley and John Gilbert stayed at the Angel in Stretford while work proceeded. Once the canal was open, local produce, especially rhubarb and vegetables from Stretford, could be shipped into Manchester much more quickly and cheaply, to the benefit of the local farms. This is the view from Edge Lane Bridge looking towards Manchester in the 1970s. The area on the left just out of the picture used to be the coal wharf where barges full of coal from Worsley would unload. For some years there was even a packet boat which operated from Manchester to Lymm and onwards, and for 6*d* you could go from here to Manchester on a boat pulled by two strong horses.

The Manchester Ship Canal was formed by deepening and developing the River Irwell which ran along the northern border of Stretford. When the Canal opened in 1894 it brought the world to Stretford, and a number of wharfs developed within the area, mostly on the southern bank, including the Co-operative Society Wharf. The dry docks, still working today, are definitely in Stretford. This photograph from 1949 shows Barton Locks with the ships *Pacific Enterprise* and *Sculptor* being manoeuvred by tugs in and out of the locks. The smaller lock enabled the tug to go through the lock at the same time as the larger boat it was towing.

The next transport upheaval was the arrival of the railways in 1849. The line to Altrincham was something of an after-thought to the line from London Road station to the junction with the Liverpool line, and thus the Manchester South Junction & Altrincham Railway was created. The railway through Stretford encouraged businesses to come into the area, and it also meant the spread of houses for the new commuter population which settled in Stretford. In the postwar years, in addition to the Altrincham electric train, steam trains ran to Chester, stopping at Stretford, Timperley and Altrincham. This is LMS tank engine no. 40006 at Timperley, on a stopping train to Chester in 1945. (Photo: Locofotos)

There were five stations in Stretford: Old Trafford (Trafford Bar), Warwick Road (opened in 1931), Stretford (on the Altrincham line), Manchester United Halt and Trafford Park (Moss Road) on the Liverpool Central line. But there was also another railway in Stretford: this line ran from Central station (where it joined the Liverpool line) under Ayres Road, Kings Road and Ryebank Road through to Chorlton station and on to Stockport and the south. This line was used for goods only for many years after Chorlton station was closed. The unused trackbed is now earmarked for one of the Metrolink extensions. Here, Easter Region no. 63868 hauls a coal train through Chorlton towards Trafford Park, September 1954. (Photo: Locofotos)

Stretford station, 1970. The buildings and waiting rooms are being dismantled and the station has a dilapidated air about it. Today it is a Metrolink station, but looks even worse – the building on Edge Lane is very run down.

Warwick Road station on the Altrincham line, 1975. It used to have four platforms to enable it to deal with the cricket crowds. There was a temporary halt here to serve the Royal Botanical Gardens Exhibition, but it was not until the line was electrified that a permanent station was erected in 1931.

Trafford Park Motive Power Depot (17F), Trafford Sheds, were situated just behind the Manchester United football ground and were entered from Railway Road. Train-spotting youngsters used to sneak in on many a Saturday morning but were promptly chased out of the shed. Here is 'Black 8' no. 48288, having just completed a goods duty, dropping ash at Trafford Park on 30 June 1962. (Photo: Locofotos)

Rebuilt Patriot class no. 45536, *Private W. Wood V.C.*, has just come off a Liverpool-Hull express in 1962. No sign of these sheds survives today. There was always an interesting mixture in these sheds, with freight engines from the Yorkshire coalfields and ER engines, mostly B1s, which handled the Parkinston Quay expresses, and even a few Britannias for the daily London train to St Pancras. (Photo: Locofotos)

A horse-drawn omnibus with an outing from the old Robin Hood Hotel on Barton Road, Stretford. Although this postcard dates from 1905, the picture itself must date from before 1899 when the old Robin Hood was taken down and the present one built.

Horse-trams arrived in Stretford in around 1880. The Manchester Carriage & Tramway Company had a terminus next to the Old Cock inn and ran a good service into Manchester, with one route going via Trafford Bar and City Road, and the next via Brooks's Bar, Hulme and All Saints'. This is one of the latter from around 1886.

A horse-tram at Trafford Bar (Talbot Road), having just arrived from Piccadilly (the Infirmary), Manchester, 1900. Horse-trams ran on the lines laid down by the Manchester Corporation until around 1902 when the Corporation began an electric tram service.

Going home time in Park Road, Stretford, in the early 1950s. Taken from the railway bridge near the fire station, this photograph shows the rush-hour traffic leaving Trafford Park. This junction, Fiveways, has since been completely redesigned and there are now traffic lights where the roundabout used to be. Derbyshire Lane East leads off at the top left.

The time is five minutes past five, on a working day in February 1963; the place is Westinghouse Road.
The buses, filled with workers on their way home, are waiting to turn into Trafford Park Road. In 1920
Metrovicks were asked if female workers could go out five minutes before the men so that they could get
on the trams or buses without being pushed and jostled. Metrovicks refused on the grounds that some
girls might go five minutes early and then walk or cycle home. There were 'Ladies Only' buses though:
one went to Salford and one went into Manchester each night.

The Urmston Lane/Stretford Road junction on the M62 motorway, only two lanes wide at this point,
pictured soon after it was opened in October 1962. Urmston parish church is visible on the skyline to the
left.

POSTSCRIPT

Stretford has changed a great deal over its years as a Local Board, a UDC and then a Borough. There were housing booms, schools came and went and the Arndale Centre arrived. But underneath it all there has been little change: the Bridgewater Canal still runs through the area and over the River Mersey which still controls the southern end of Stretford.

The Trafford Development, photographed in March 1997. How much will this massive shopping complex affect our lives? Will traffic jams bring Stretford to a halt? Will the Stretford Arndale die a slow death? Do we really need another ten-screen cinema complex? We will have to wait and see what happens. This area used to be called Dumplington after a local farm, but planners and whizz kids didn't like it. So it is now called the Trafford Shopping Development – a much better name. (Photo: Bill Newton)

Gorse Hill Park gates on Chester Road. These gates to the Trafford Estates used to stand opposite the spot where the White City gates are today. I can remember people living in the lovely stone-built lodges, though I do not know if they were families or park-keepers. The Trafford family Coat of Arms is above the entrance. (Photo: Bill Newton)

Hidden in the bushes on the left of the gates is the Great Stone of Stretford. This gave Greatstone Road its name, and there was also a Great Stone Farm next to Gausehill Farm in the area that is now a school. Some say the stone was used to 'purify' money during the various plagues: the holes were filled with vinegar and money left there to pay Stretford's farmers for the supplies they left for the city's inhabitants. That may be so, but the stone is of a type of rock not naturally occurring in this area. Perhaps it was brought here by the Romans to mark the ford across the River Mersey at Crossford Bridge, and was moved many years later during the Black Death. But I do not think we will ever really know. Sadly, it has lost its plaque and lies almost forgotten. (Photo: Bill Newton)

The view along Chester Road towards Manchester, from the site of Rylands' Coffee House. The road is wide enough for six lanes of traffic and two pull-ins. St Ann's Church steeple is just visible among the street lamps; the Civic Hall Tower is partly hidden behind one. (Photo: Bill Newton)

Outside Manchester United Football Ground at the score board end is this splendid memorial. The plaque records the players, officials and sports writers who died in the terrible crash in Munich. Below it is a wonderful, life-like statue of a man who came through that tragedy, and made Manchester United famous the world over: Sir Matt Busby. Apparently the hollow statue is filled with letters, cards, and souvenirs left outside the ground when his death was announced. (Photo: Bill Newton)

King Street today, a mere shadow of its former self. Argos and Buckingham's Bingo now occupy the site where the old Trafford Arms, then Wakefields shop and finally Raw's Chemist stood. The post office on the right has survived the upheaval, as has the NatWest Bank as well. (Photo: Bill Newton)

One of the boundary markers for the Gorse Hill area. Perhaps someone should have told the designers that if the letters are the same colour as the brick, they would not stand out! I was told that they cost over £4,000 to design, make and erect. (Photo: Bill Newton)

To order any of these titles please telephone our distributor, Littlehampton Book Services on 01903 721
For a catalogue of these and our other titles please ring Regina Schinner on 01453 731114